W9-DEF-371

THE SUMMER PALACE

颐 和 园

FOREIGN LANGUAGES PRESS   BEIJING

外文出版社   北京

THE SUMMER PALACE

Situated in the northwest suburbs of Beijing, the famous imperial garden Yiheyuan (Garden of Nurtured Harmony, known as the Summer Palace in the West) was originally called Qingyiyuan (Garden of Clear Ripples). It was constructed in 1750, the 15th year of the reign of Qing Dynasty Emperor Qian Long, under orders of the emperor to celebrate his mother's 60th birthday. In 1860, the 10th year of the reign of Emperor Xian Feng, Qingyiyuan was burned down by British and French allied forces. In 1886, the 12th year of the reign of Emperor Guang Xu, it was reconstructed on orders of Empress Dowager Ci Xi with funds meant for the navy, and was renamed Yiheyuan in 1888. In 1900 Yiheyuan was again devastated by the Eight-Power Allied Forces sent by Britain, the United States, Germany, France, tsarist Russia, Japan, Italy and Austria. It was restored in 1903 and officially opened as a public park in 1924.

The Summer Palace consists primarily of Wanshoushan (Longevity Hill) and Kunming Lake. Of its 2.9-square-kilometer area, water covers three-fourths. The ancient buildings cover an area of nearly 70.000 square meters.

Based on the natural hills and water courses. most of the buildings in the Summer Palace reflect scenic spots and historical sites south of the Yangtze River. These colorful and majestic wonders include pavilions. bridges. corridors. halls and palaces.

On the south face of Longevity Hill. the glittering Paiyundian(Cloud-Dispelling Hall) complex topped with yellow glazed tiles and set among green pines and cypresses resembles the moon surrounded by a myriad of stars. This resplendent and magnificent group of buildings. from the shore to the hilltop. consist of a decorated archway. Paiyunmen (Cloud-Dispelling Gate). Ergongmen (The Second Palace Gate). Paiyundian. Dehuidian (Hall of Virtuous Light). Foxiangge (Pagoda of Buddhist Incense). and Zhihuihai (Wisdom-Sea Temple). The Pagoda of Buddhist Incense. a three-story octagonal building. sitting on the hill and facing Kunming Lake. dominates the entire garden. Zhuanlunzang (Revolving Scripture Repository) and the large stela dedicated to Longevity Hill and Kunming Lake stand on its east face; Wufangge (Five-Direction Pavilions) and the world-famous Baoyunge (Precious Cloud Pavilion). also called Tongdian (Bronze Pavilion). on its west terrace. Viewed from the Pagoda of Buddhist Incense. Xidi(West Causeway). which was constructed in imitation of Su Dyke on Hangzhou's West Lake. looks like a green ribbon unwinding from south to north on Kunming Lake. Each of the six bridges on the West Causeway has its own form and each is graceful in its own way. Looking like a rainbow. the Seventeen-Arch Bridge is captivating.

lying on the lake in mists. Hanxutang (Hall of Forbearance and Humbleness), Zaojian Hall and Zhijing Hall stand like three legs of a tripod on the water, recalling the "three fabled abodes of immortals at sea" in Chinese folk tales. By the lake, the famous Marble Boat, the lifelike bronze ox, a symbol of successful flood control, and the Zhichunting (Pavilion Heralding Spring) are the major points of interest.

On the north face of Longevity Hill with its wavy terrain, luxuriant and well-spaced flowers and trees, winding hill paths, and towering pines and cypresses, the building complex designed in the style of Tibetan temples stands magnificently dignified. At the foot of Longevity Hill, the pure water of the lake flows east quietly and slowly. The replica of an old-fashioned business street laid out along the back lake, which follows the typical architectural style of market places along rivers in South China, contains a variety of orderly arranged commercial establishments, such as banks, drugstores, teahouses and pubs. If one samples a cup of top-grade tea in a boat on the lake while enjoying the story telling and ballad singing in Suzhou dialect, he will feel as if he was in old Suzhou in Jiangsu Province. Walking north along the creek to the end, one will find Xiequyuan (Garden of Harmonious Delight), an exquisite structure with buildings, halls, covered corridors and pavilions ingeniously interconnected around a pond formed by water from Kunming Lake.

The Summer Palace with its unmatched scenery is the most heart-cheering place in Beijing. It is a milestone in the history of Chinese garden construction, epitomizing the cream of Chinese gardening art.

颐 和 园

颐和园位于北京市西北郊,原名清漪园,始建于公元 1750 年(清乾隆十五年),是清朝乾隆皇帝为其母祝六十寿辰而建造的一座以湖光山色蜚声于世的大型皇家园林。1860 年(清咸丰十年)清漪园被英法联军焚毁。1886 年(清光绪十二年)慈禧太后挪用海军经费,在清漪园废墟上重新修建并于 1888 年改园名为颐和园。1900 年,又遭英、美、德、法、俄、日、意、奥八国联军抢掠破坏,1903 年重修。1924 年正式辟为公园。

颐和园主要由万寿山和昆明湖组成,全园面积约 2.9 平方公里,其中水面占四分之三左右。园内古建筑 3000 余间,面积近 7 万平方米。

颐和园园林布局以自然山水为基础,其建筑结构多模拟江南名胜古迹,或肖其意,或仿其型,因地制宜地创建了众多绚丽多彩、壮丽恢宏的亭、桥、廊、榭,殿、宇、楼、台。

万寿山南麓,黄色琉璃瓦顶的排云殿建筑群在郁郁苍苍的松柏簇拥下似众星捧月,溢彩流光。这组金碧辉煌的建筑自湖边的云辉玉宇牌楼起，经排云门、二宫门、排云殿、德辉殿、佛香阁，直至山巅的智慧海，重廊复殿，层层叠叠，气势磅礴。巍峨高耸的佛香阁八面三层，踞山面湖，统领全园。其东面山石上有转轮藏和高大的万寿山昆明湖石碑，西侧台基上是五方阁与闻名中外的宝云阁铜殿。登上佛香阁，凭栏纵目，碧波荡漾的昆明湖上，仿杭州西湖苏堤建造的西堤，犹如一条绿色的飘带，蜿蜒曲折，纵贯南北。堤上六座桥，造型互异，婀娜多姿。浩淼烟波中，十七孔桥似长虹偃月横卧水面，涵虚堂、藻鉴堂、治镜阁三座水中岛屿鼎足而立，寓意神话传说中的"海山三山"。在湖畔岸边，还建有著名的石舫，维妙维肖的镇水铜牛，赏春观景的知春亭等点景建筑。

万寿山北麓，山势起伏，花木扶疏，道路幽邃，松柏参天。重峦叠嶂上，仿西藏寺庙构筑的四大部洲建筑群层台耸立，雄伟庄严。山脚下，清澈的湖水随山型地貌演变为一条宁静舒缓的河流，宛转而东去。河两岸模拟江南水肆建造的买卖街，铺面鳞次栉比，钱庄、药店招幌临风；茶楼、酒馆画旗斜矗。若轻摇画舫，品碧螺香茗，听一曲苏州评弹，使人如临姑苏之乡。沿河游览，水尽之处，有小巧玲珑的谐趣园，该园结构精致，楼堂廊榭皆环池而立，"一亭一径，足谐奇趣。"

"何处燕山最畅情，无双风月属昆明。"颐和园集中国历代造园艺术之精粹，是中国园林艺术史上的里程碑。古往今来，她以其杰出的园林艺术成就倾倒了无数中外游客，被人们赞誉为"人间天堂"。

Yanxiu Pailou (Gathering Elegance Archway)

Built in 1750, the archway has four pillars and seven roofs arranged in three layers. The Chinese characters inscribed on the horizontal stone tablet were written by Emperor Qian Long (reigned 1736-1795). It is the largest decorated archway surviving from the Qing Dynasty.

罢秀牌楼

建于 1750 年，四柱七楼，主楼石额题刻为乾隆皇帝（公元 1736-1795 年在位）御笔，是清代保存至今最大的一座过街牌楼。

◁ Donggongmen（Eastern Palace Gate）

This was the entrance to the Summer Palace used by the emperor and empress during the Qing Dynasty. A gold horizontal tablet is hung on the lintel above the gate inscribed with the three Chinese characters "Yiheyuan" in the calligraphy of Emperor Guang Xu（reigned 1875-1908）. The stone carved with two dragons playing with a pearl inlaid in the footstep is from the remains of Yuanmingyuan（Garden of Perfect Brightness）.

东宫门

是清代帝后出入颐和园的正门。宫门悬挂着光绪皇帝（公元 1875-1908 年在位）题写的"颐和园"金匾。台阶中间镶嵌的二龙戏珠石雕，是圆明园遗物。

Renshoudian
（Hall of Benevolence and Longevity）

This was the hall where the emperor and Empress Dowager Ci Xi conducted state affairs and received senior officials while staying at the Summer Palace. This seven-bay-wide structure was covered by a rooftop in *xieshan* style with grey tiles. Bronze phoenixes and dragons were placed in front of the hall to represent royal power.

仁寿殿

是清代帝后驻园期间听政理事之所，大殿灰瓦歇山顶，面阔七间，殿前月台上排列着铜凤、铜龙等吉祥物，具有权力的象征。

Inside the Hall of Benevolence and Longevity

While holding audiences with senior officials，Empress Dowager Ci Xi sat on the throne at the center of the hall with Emperor Guang Xu beside her on another chair. The red-crowned crane and censer are placed as they were in the Qing Court.

仁寿殿内景

当年慈禧太后接见大臣时，坐在殿内正中的宝座上，而光绪皇帝则坐在旁边临时安放的坐椅上。殿内安放的仙鹤、香炉等物品皆为清室原物陈列。

Zhichunting (Pavilion Heralding Spring)

Standing on an islet, this pavilion was built during the reign of Emperor Qian Long. In Emperor Guang Xu's reign, it was connected to the shore by a bridge. It is the best place to appreciate the Summer Palace in spring.

知春亭

乾隆时原是水中的一座小岛，光绪时修桥梁与湖岸相连，是观赏园林春色的最佳处。

Wenchangge (Pavilion of Cultural Prosperity)
Located on the eastern bank of Kunming Lake, this is a two-story city-gate tower. Bronze sculptures of God of Literature (a god in Daoist legend) and his horse were placed here for worship.

文昌阁
位于昆明湖东岸,是一座两层楼阁式样的城关建筑,阁上供奉文昌帝君(道教神名之一)及其坐骑铜像。

Long-distance view of Kunming Lake and Pagoda of Buddhist Incense
远眺昆明湖、佛香阁

Shuimuziqin (Hall of Affinity Between Water and Wood)

This was the main entrance to the Empress Dowager's residence chambers. The horizontal tablet above the gate was inscribed with the four Chinese characters "Shuimuziqin." In front of the hall, there is a wharf built to satisfy the Empress Dowager's need to go boating on Kunming Lake, and a large frame used to hang gas lamps.

水木自亲

当年慈禧太后寝宫的正门。门前临水建有码头,专供慈禧太后游湖乘船使用。门前有一巨型灯架,过去用来悬挂汽灯,俗称"水月灯竿"。

Yulantang (Hall of Jade Ripples)

This was the private living quarters of Emperor Guang Xu while he stayed at the Summer Palace. The western hall was his bedroom and the eastern hall his study. Following the failure of the Reform Movement of 1898, the Emperor Dowager had the emperor imprisoned here.

玉澜堂

光绪皇帝驻园时的寝宫。大殿西为寝室，东为书房。1898年，"戊戌变法"失败后，慈禧太后来园时便将光绪皇帝囚禁在此。

Purple Magnolia ▷

This magnolia tree was planted in the backyard of the Hall of Joyful Longevity over 200 years ago.

紫玉兰

植于乐寿堂后院,已有 200 年以上树龄。

Leshoutang (Hall of Joyful Longevity)

This luxuriously furnished residence chambers belonged to Empress Dowager Ci Xi. The western suite was her bedroom, the eastern suite her dressing room, and the central hall the place where she conducted state affairs and had her meals.

乐寿堂

慈禧太后的寝宫。殿内装饰华美,陈设奢侈。大殿西侧套间是卧室,东侧套间是更衣室,正厅中间宝座是慈禧太后临时理政及用膳的地方。

大清國慈禧皇太后

Portrait of Empress Dowager Ci Xi

Dutch painter Hubert Vos created this oil painting for 71-year-old Empress Dowager in the Summer Palace in 1905. It is now in the Qinghuaxuan (House of Elegant Flowers).

慈禧太后画像

1905 年荷兰画家华士胡博在颐和园为 71 岁的慈禧太后绘制了此幅油画像。现置于清华轩内。

Qingzhixiu (Blue-Iris Hill)

This is also called Ruin-A-Family Stone. According to the historical record, during the Ming Dynasty an official named Mi Wanzhong found this stone in Fangshan in southwestern Beijing and wanted to move it to Shaoyuan (now in Beijing University). However, he had to abandon it at Liangxiang after spending all his money trying to transport it. In 1751 Emperor Qian Long found the rock on the road while visiting the south and had it moved to the Summer Palace. Later he had some poems carved on it as a eulogy.

青芝岫

又名败家石。史料记载,明代官吏米万钟在北京房山觅得此石后,欲运往勺园(今北京大学内),终因耗资巨大而财力衰竭,半途而废弃至良乡。1751年,乾隆皇帝南巡时,见到此石,命人运至园内并在石上多处镌刻赞美此石的诗句。

Yangrenfeng (Wind of Virtue)
Also known as the Fan Hall, it is located west of the Hall of Joyful Longevity. The floor and the articles within are all fan-shaped, hence the name Fan Hall.

扬仁风
东临乐寿堂,建筑平面及殿内陈设品皆为扇面式样,俗称扇面殿。

◁

The Great Stage
Built in 1891, it is 21 metres high and consists of three levels. The stage at the lowest level is 17 metres wide. Opera may be performed simultaneously on all three levels of the stage.

大戏楼
建于 1891 年,戏楼三层,高 21 米,底层舞台宽 17 米。三层可同时演出大型戏剧。

Yiledian (Hall of Nurtured Joy)
Opposite the Great Stage, this was where Empress Dowager Ci Xi watched theatrical performances while sitting on her gold- and enamel-inlad sandalwood throne.

颐乐殿
位于戏楼对面,内安放着红木金漆珐琅宝座,是专供慈禧太后看戏用的。

Changlang (Long Promenade)

Skirting the northern bank of Kunming Lake on the southern side of Longevity Hill, the Long Promenade is one of the Summer Palace's major structures. It is 728 meters long and has 273 bays, including four double-eaved octagon pavilions which symbolize the four seasons of the year. The promenade is decorated with nearly 10,000 paintings of human figures, flowers, and landscapes.

长廊

位于昆明湖北岸,万寿山南麓,是颐和园内的主要建筑之一。全长728米,共273间。廊中有四座象征四季的重檐八角亭,廊亭内绘有近万幅人物典故、花卉山水等彩画。

Yunhuiyuyu Pailou

This waterside wooden archway with four pillars and seven roofs in three layers was built in the 15th year of the reign of Emperor Qian Long (1750) and reconstructed during the reign of Emperor Guang Xu. The four characters "yunhuiyuyu" inscribed on its front side mean "Gorgeous Clouds and Jade Palace."

云辉玉宇牌楼

是一座临水的四柱七楼木结构牌楼，始建于清乾隆十五年(公元 1750 年)，光绪时重建。

Cloud-Dispelling Hall Scenic Area ▷

This is the main building complex of the Summer Palace. From the Yunhuiyuyu Pailou at the shore of Kunming Lake to the Wisdom-Sea Temple on the top of Longevity Hill, the plan of this building complex suits the terrain and demonstrates layers of exact symmetry. The yellow roofs of glazed tiles make the central halls even more beautiful and splendid.

排云殿景区

颐和园内的主景建筑群。从湖岸云辉玉宇牌楼起，至万寿山山顶智慧海，建筑布局严谨对称，依山顺势，层层叠叠。中央殿宇采用黄色琉璃瓦顶显得更加富丽堂皇。

◁ Paiyundian（Cloud-Dispelling Hall）

The main structure in the building complex on the southern slope of Longevity Hill. Every year on Empress Dowager Ci Xi's birthday she sat in the padauk throne decorated with carved dragons, receiving congratulations from Emperor Guang Xu and princes, dukes and ministers. Most of the articles displayed in the hall were birthday presents given to Ci Xi by members of the nobility.

排云殿

万寿山南麓的主要建筑之一。过去每逢慈禧太后过生日时便坐在殿内紫檀雕龙宝座上，接受光绪皇帝及王公大臣的贺拜。现殿内陈设的文物多是当年王公大臣送给慈禧太后的寿礼。

Inside the Cloud-Dispelling Hall
排云殿内景

Zhuanlunzang (Revolving Scripture Repository)

A complex of religious buildings to the east of the Pagoda of Buddhist Incense. In front of the tower is a large stela dedicated to Longevity Hill and Kunming Lake which is inscribed on the back with a short essay about the construction of Kunming Lake written by Emperor Qian Long.

转轮藏

位于佛香阁东侧,是一组宗教建筑。楼前竖立的"万寿山昆明湖"石碑上,镌刻着乾隆皇帝手书有关兴建昆明湖的碑文。

Wufangge (Five-Direction Pavilions)

A religious building complex to the west of the Pagoda of Buddhist Incense. On the huge white marble terrace in the center stands the well-known bronze pavilion, the Pavilion of Precious Cloud, which is 7.55 meters high, weighs 207 tons and is beautifully elaborated with complex workmanship.

五方阁

是一宗教建筑,在佛香阁西侧。阁前正中巨大的汉白玉石台上,矗立着著名的宝云阁铜殿,高 7.55 米,重 207 吨,工艺繁复,精美绝伦。

Statue of Bodhisattva

This gilded bronze Statue of Bodhisattva was cast in the reign of Ming Emperor Wan Li (1573-1620). It was first housed in the Mituo Temple in Beijing and later moved to the Pagoda of Buddhist Incense.

千手观音

铜胎鎏金千手观音铸于明代万历年间(公元 1573－1620 年)，原置北京弥陀寺，后移放于佛香阁内。

Foxiangge
(Pagoda of Buddhist Incense)

This pagoda was originally designed after the nine-story Six Harmony Pagoda (Liuheta) on the banks of the Qiantang River in Hangzhou. Emperor Qian Long later had it rebuilt as a three-story, octagon tower with a quadruple-eaved roof. The top of the 41-meter-high pagoda offers a spectacular view.

佛香阁

原是仿杭州钱塘江畔六和塔建造的九层宝塔，后被乾隆皇帝拆改为三层八面四重檐的木结构楼阁。阁高 41 米，登临远眺，四围风光，一览无余。

Zhihuihai (Wisdom-Sea Temple)

Built entirely of brick and stone, this structure was known as the "beamless hall," in which a bronze statue of Guanyin cast in the 15th year of the reign of Emperor Qian Long (1750) was consecrated. There are 1,110 exquisitely glazed Buddha statuettes set in the outer wall of the hall.

智慧海

用砖石发券砌成,俗称无梁殿。殿内供奉着一尊乾隆十五年(公元 1750 年)铸造的观音铜像。殿外楼壁上镶嵌着 1110 尊造型精美的琉璃小佛像。

A bird's-eye view of the Pagoda ▷ of Buddhist Incense

佛香阁俯瞰

Sunset on Kunming Lake
昆明湖夕阳

Pleasure Boat in the Lake
This boat, called "Taihe," is modelled on Emperor Qian Long's dragon boat.

湖中画舫
"太和号"画舫是仿乾隆皇帝当年乘坐的龙船制造的。

◁ Tower of Rising Rosy Clouds

Located at the east foot of Longevity Hill, this tower serves as a pass for the northeast corner of the Summer Palace.

赤城霞起城关

位于万寿山东麓,是颐和园东北隅的关隘。

Xiequyuan (Garden of Harmonious Delights)

At the east foot of Longevity Hill, it was originally known as Huishan Garden when it was built in 1751 in imitation of the Garden of Ease of Mind (Jichangyuan) at the piedmont of Huishan Hill in Wuxi. In the garden, a winding veranda joins the halls, pavilions, and houses, which embrace a pond. It was so exquisitely made that it rivalled the beauty of the garden in south China.

谐趣园

在万寿山东麓,原名惠山园。是 1751 年仿无锡惠山脚下的寄畅园建造的。园内弯曲的游廊,连接着殿、堂、轩、榭,环池而立,构造巧妙,极尽江南园林之趣。

Zhiyuqiao（Know-Your-Fish Bridge）

On the archway at the start of the bridge are carved poems composed by Emperor Qian Long while he was enjoying the sight of the fish in the water.

知鱼桥

是谐趣园内的景点,桥头牌楼上镌刻着乾隆皇帝观鱼取乐的诗句。

◁

House of Clear Water and Cool Breeze, Fresh View Tower

Located in the Garden of Harmonious Delights, they served as spots where emperors and empresses stopped to sit and admire the view during walks in the garden.

澄爽斋、瞩新楼

座落在谐趣园内,是帝后在园内游乐时,观景休息的地方。

◁ The Glazed Tile Pagoda of Many Treasures

This pagoda was built using five-color glazed bricks and tiles, and is 16 meters high with three stories and a seven-eaved roof. On each story are glazed Buddha statues inlaid in the wall. The pagoda looks magnificent and dignified standing in the pine woods and cypresses east of the north face of Longevity Hill.

多宝琉璃塔

用五色琉璃砖瓦砌成，高 16 米，三层七重檐，每层镶嵌琉璃佛像，华丽庄严，耸立在万寿山北麓迤东的松柏之中。

Sidabuzhou（The Four Great Regions）

A large complex of religious buildings on the north slope of Longevity Hill, they were built by Emperor Qian Long imitating the structure of Tibetan-style temples. The buildings include the Terrace of the Sun, Terrace of the Moon, Four Great Regions, and Eight Small Regions.

四大部洲

位于万寿山北麓，这组规模宏大的宗教建筑，是乾隆皇帝仿西藏寺庙构造的。主要由日台、月台、四大部洲、八小部洲等组成。

Suzhoujie (Suzhou Street)

Also known as Business Street, it is located on both sides of the Back Stream at the northern foot of Longevity Hill. This is a commercial street built by Emperor Qian Long for his mother's birthday, and is modelled on the streets in the region of rivers and lakes in south China. The street was burned down in 1860 by the British and French allied forces and rebuilt in 1989. Suzhou Street is over 300 meters long and is lined by more than 60 shops such as old-style private banks, wineshops, teahouses, shoe shops, etc.

苏州街

又称买卖街,位于万寿山北麓后溪河两岸,是乾隆皇帝为其母祝寿,仿江南水乡建造的一条商业街市。1860 年被英法联军焚毁,1989 年重建。水街全长 300 余米,有钱庄、酒馆、茶楼、鞋店等铺面 60 余处。

Towering Pines and Cypresses
On the north slope of Longevity Hill are many winding paths along which several hundred pines and cypresses nearly 300 years old stand as a record of the famous garden's rise and decline, honor and disgrace.

松柏参天
万寿山北麓曲径通幽，数百棵近 300 年树龄的古松柏记载着名园的兴衰、荣辱。

◁ **The Back Stream**
Here is a clear, tranquil creek with jagged rocks and verdant woods on either bank, also known as Suzhou Creek.

后溪河
清幽宁静，两岸山石嶙峋，树木葱郁。

Suyunyan Tower

The tower stands on the west of Longevity Hill where on the tower a statue of Guan Yu was dedicated. This echoes the Pavilion of Cultural Prosperity at a distance east of the lake, symbolizing literature on the left and martial arts on the right.

宿云檐城关

万寿山西面的关口，楼上原供奉关羽塑像，它与湖东岸的文昌阁遥相呼应，有左文右武之意。

Xingqiao (Bridge of Floating Heart)

The bridge spans the Little Suzhou Creek to the west of the Marble Boat with a towering four-post archway at each end. The inscriptions on the archways were written by Emperor Qian Long.

荇桥

横跨石舫西侧小苏州河上，桥东西各有一座四柱冲天牌楼，楼额为乾隆皇帝御笔。

Shifang（Marble Boat）

Also known as Qingyan Boat，it is 36 meters long and made of huge marble slabs．When first built in 1755 it was a two-storied boat in the Chinese style，but it was destroyed by the British and French allied forces in 1860．In 1893 it was redone as a western-style pleasure boat by adding stone wheels.

石舫

又名清晏舫，船体长 36 米，用巨大石块雕砌而成。1755 年初建时为两层中式楼船，1860 年被英法联军烧毁。1893 年仿外国游轮在石船两侧添加石轮改为洋式楼船。

Tingliguan（Listen-to-the-Orioles Hall）

In this hall is a small stage where Emperor Qian Long enjoyed watching performances. It is now a restaurant serving court cuisine.

听鹂馆

馆内有乾隆皇帝看戏的小戏楼。现已辟为品尝宫庭御膳的场所。

Pavilion Covering the Hill and Lake Scenery

This three-story pavilion is connected with the west section of the Long Promenade. When one ascends it and looks afar, the hill and the lake come into view.

山色湖光共一楼

是连接长廊的一座三层楼阁。登楼远眺，山光水色，尽收眼底。

Huazhongyou (Scenic Stroll) ▷

Standing on the hill to the north of Listen-to-the-Orioles Hall, this spot consists of pavilions, corridors, towers and stone archways. Walking through its corridors and lingering about its towers is like strolling through a picture.

画中游

耸立在听鹂馆北面山石上，由亭、廊、楼、阁、石牌楼等组成，人游其间，穿廊驻阁，如历画中。

Jadeite Table Plaque

Made in the Qing Dynasty, it is 44.4 cm high, 38.1 cm wide, and 0.7 cm thick.

翡翠插屏

清代,高 44.4 厘米,宽 38.1 厘米,厚 0.7 厘米,为颐和园旧藏。

◁

Sanxi *Zun* (wine container)

Cast in the 16 century B.C. during the Shang Dynasty, this exquisitely made 63.2 cm-tall wine container is a national treasure.

三牺尊

商,公元前 1500 年左右,高 63.2 厘米。铸造精美,堪称国宝。

Empress Dowager Ci Xi's Car
The oldest surviving imported automobile in China, with a three-cylinder engine and "DURYEA" carved on the stirrup. This car was made by the Duryea motor wagon company of America.

慈禧太后御用汽车
为中国现存最早的进口汽车。采用三缸式发动机，车镫上铸有英文 DURYEA，此车为美国图利亚兄弟公司制造。

A Distant View of the Pagoda of Buddhist Incense from the West Causeway

西堤远眺佛香阁

◁ Liuqiao (Willow Bridge)
One of the six bridges at the West Causeway.

柳桥
西堤六桥之一。

Sunset clouds over Binfeng Bridge
豳风桥夕云

Yudaiqiao（Jade Belt Bridge）
玉带桥

Jingqiao（Mirror Bridge）
波光堤影赏镜桥

◁ **Lianqiao（Belt Bridge）in snow**
  雪中练桥

Zhijing Tower（Site of Zhijingge）
On an isle in the western part of Kunming lake. A castle-style tower once stood there.

治镜阁遗址
原为昆明湖西湖湖心岛上的一座城堡式水城。

Jingminglou (Jingming Tower)

Built in the pattern of Yueyang Tower in Hunan Province during Emperor Qian Long's reign, it was destroyed by the British and French allied forces in 1860 and rebuilt in 1990.

景明楼

乾隆皇帝时仿湖南岳阳楼建造。1860 年被英法联军烧毁，1990 年重建。

Seventeen-Arch Bridge

This bridge connects Kuoruting (Pavilion of Broad View) in the east and the South Lake Isle in the west. It is the longest stone bridge in any Chinese garden with a span of 150 meters. The bridge railings are decorated with 544 vividly carved stone lions.

十七孔桥

东连廓如亭,西接南湖岛,全长 150 米,是中国古代园林中最长的石桥。桥栏望柱上雕刻了 544 只形态生动的小石狮。

△
Hanxutang (Hall of Forbearance and Humbleness)
Originally this was the three-storied Watching the Moon Tower. It was later rebuilt as a one-story building. The Qing emperors and empresses used to inspect drills of waterborne forces here.

涵虚堂
原为三层望蟾阁,后改建为一层。清代帝后曾在这里检阅水军操练。

Dragon King Statue
This image was originally consecrated in the Dragon King's Temple of Kunming Lake. Since the lake is located in west Beijing, this is said to be the Dragon King of the West Sea.

龙王像
昆明湖中旧有龙王庙,因湖在京城西方,所以在庙内供奉西海龙王。

Kuoruting（Pavilion of Broad View）
The pavilion is an octagon building with a double-eaved pointed roof. Hung on the eight sides of the pavilion are boards inscribed with poems and prose in the handwriting of Emperor Qian Long and his ministers.

廓如亭

八方重檐攒尖顶,亭内八面悬挂着乾隆皇帝及大臣手书诗文匾。

◁ **Bronze Ox**
The bronze ox was cast in the 20th year of Emperor Qian Long's reign (1755). On the back of the ox is the "Golden Ox Inscription" in seal characters, a style of Chinese calligraphy often used on seals, written by Emperor Qian Long. The ox is fashioned in a realistic style.

镇水铜牛

铸造于清乾隆二十年(公元 1755 年),牛背上铭铸乾隆皇帝御制"金牛铭"篆书。神态逼真,栩栩如生。

A Map of the Western Suburbs of Beijing Created in the Qing Dynasty

清代绘制的北京西郊名胜图

图书在版编目(CIP)数据

颐和园:英汉对照/兰佩瑾编:姚天新文。—北京:外文出版社,1997
ISBN 7-119-02036-6

Ⅰ.颐…Ⅱ.①兰…②姚…Ⅲ.颐和园-摄影集　Ⅳ.J426.1
中国版本图书馆 CIP 数据核字(96)第 25613 号

Edited by：Lan Peijin
Text by：Yao Tianxin
Photos by：Yao Tianxin
Translated by：Xu Rong　Li Jing
Bookcover designed by：Tang Shaowen
Plates designed by：Yuan Qing

编辑：兰佩瑾
撰文：姚天新
摄影：姚天新
翻译：许　荣　李　晶
封面设计：唐少文
图版设计：元　青

颐和园

兰佩瑾 编

Ⓒ　外文出版社
外文出版社出版
(中国北京百万庄大街 24 号)
邮政编码100037
深圳当纳利旭日印刷有限公司印刷
1997 年(24 开)第一版
1997 年第一版第一次印刷

ISBN 7-119-02036-6/J・1397
003900（精）

The Summer Palace

ISBN 7-119-02036-6

Ⓒ　Foreign Languages Press
Published by Foreign Languages Press
24 Baiwanzhuang Road，Beijing 100037，China
Printed in the People's Republic of China